W9-CXO-311

TABLE OF CONTENTS

―――――➤►◄―――――

Unless otherwise indicated, all Scripture quotations are taken from the *King James Version* of the Bible.

SECRETS OF THE JOURNEY, VOLUME 7
ISBN 1-56394-065-5
Copyright © 1997 by *MIKE MURDOCK*
All publishing rights belong exclusively to Wisdom International
Published by The Wisdom Center · P. O. Box 99 · Denton, Texas 76202
1-888-WISDOM-1 (1-888-947-3661) · Website: www.thewisdomcenter.cc

The Secret Of Your Future
Is Hidden
In Your Daily Routine.

-MIKE MURDOCK

❧ 1 ❧

Establish Your Personal Secret Place For Meeting Daily With The Holy Spirit.

━━━━●━━━━

The Secret Place Is The Place Where You Meet With God Every Day Of Your Life.

It is where you enter His presence and become changed, informed, corrected and loved. It is the room where you kneel in humility at the altar of mercy and receive forgiveness, restoration and revelation regarding your Assignment on earth.

It is your prayer room, the prayer closet, or *any place* you have sanctified and set apart for the *exclusive use of the Holy Spirit* to deal privately and intimately with your life.

This focus on *The Secret Place* is possibly the most life changing, revolutionizing teaching you may hear during your lifetime, if you discern the dramatic encounters such a place can birth.

15 Keys To Entering The Secret Place

1. *Enter Daily.* The Psalmist said, "Lord, I have called daily upon Thee, I have stretched out my hands unto Thee" (Ps. 88:9).

2. *Enter With Expectation.* God honors it. "...for he that cometh to God must believe that He is, and that He is a rewarder of them that diligently seek Him" (Heb. 11:6).

Expectation is a current. It sweeps you into the Holy Place. It brings you into God's presence where you are purged, purified and changed.

▶ Expect God to *respond* to you.

▶ Expect pain to *leave* your body.

▶ Expect *confusion* to depart from your mind.

▶ Expect *revelation* concerning those you love to come to you.

▶ Expect *change* when you enter God's presence.

▶ Expect supernatural *peace* and joy to explode within your heart as you enter His presence.

3. *Enter Before Making Financial Decisions.* The Apostle Paul understood this. "But my God shall supply all your need according to His riches in glory by Christ Jesus" (Phil. 4:19).

4. *Enter Confessing Your Weaknesses And Expect To Be Made Strong.* Jesus is your difference. "I can do all things through Christ which strengtheneth me" (Phil. 4:13).

5. *Enter With A Broken And Contrite Spirit.* Humility is the magnet that never fails to attract God. "The Lord is nigh unto them that are of a broken heart; and saveth such as be of a contrite spirit" (Ps. 34:18).

6. *Enter When You Feel Forsaken And All Alone.* It worked for the greatest king of Israel. "I have been young, and now am old; yet have I not

seen the righteous forsaken, nor His seed begging bread" (Ps. 37:25).

7. *Enter When You Need Mercy.* It was the mercy of David's anointing. "He is ever merciful," (Ps. 37:26).

8. *Enter When You Have Fallen Into Deep Sin And Erred.* Reaching is your remedy for sins (read Ps. 37:23,24).

9. *Enter When Slanderous Words Are Stirring Up Enemies And Strife Against You.* The arms of God are always your best defense. "Thou shalt hide them in the secret of Thy presence from the pride of man: Thou shalt keep them secretly in a pavilion from the strife of tongues" (Ps. 31:20).

10. *Enter During Seasons Of Confusion And Change.* Transition is often your most vulnerable season. "My times are in Thy hand: deliver me from the hand of mine enemies, and from them that persecute me" (Ps. 31:15).

11. *Enter When You Are Divided In Your Decision-Making And Do Not Know Which Road To Take.* Consulting God is never a mistake. "I will instruct thee and teach thee in the way which thou shalt go: I will guide thee with Mine eye" (Ps. 32:8).

12. *Enter When Bankruptcy Threatens And Poverty Is Strangling You Financially.* God wants you to prosper. "This poor man cried, and the Lord heard him, and saved him out of all his troubles" (Ps. 34:6).

13. *Enter Into The Secret Place When You Are Threatened, Abused Or Afraid.* "The angel of the Lord encampeth round about them that fear Him, and delivereth them" (Ps. 34:7).

14. *Enter Into His Presence When It Appears That Your Dreams And Goals Are Unachievable.* God loves the impossible. "O fear the Lord, ye His saints: for there is no want to them that fear Him. The young lions do lack, and suffer hunger: but they that seek the Lord shall not want any good thing" (Ps. 34:9,10).

15. *Enter Into His Presence When Everything Is Going Well And Perfect In Your Life.* The goodness of God deserves recognition. "I will bless the Lord at all times: His praise shall continually be in my mouth. My soul shall make her boast in the Lord:" (Ps. 34:1,2).

Establish Your Personal Secret Place For Meeting Daily With The Holy Spirit.

It is one of the Secrets of the Journey.

~ 2 ~

Always Pinpoint Your Goals.

Few Know What They Really Want To Do.
That is why they would change their entire plan for the day when a friend drops by the house. Their goals were not clear. They really were not sold on their goals for that day.

7 Facts About Your Dreams And Goals

1. *Nobody Can Determine Your Own Goals For You.* You must decide what generates joy in your own heart.

2. *Different People Have Different Goals.* What is important to me may be totally unimportant to another. When they get in my presence, the difference emerges.

Let me explain.

I have a dream of creating a ten-year mentorship program for parents. This consists of 120 extraordinary books. Using a chapter each day (31 keys for each 31 days of the month), I would like to create a mentorship system for parents to use with their children ages six years old to sixteen years old.

This would provide parents with a "Wisdom Encyclopedia" for their family. At breakfast each morning, they could read one chapter and mentor their children on such topics as: 31 Facts About God, 31 Facts About Jesus, 31 Facts About The Holy Spirit, 31 Facts About Angels, 31 Facts About Achieving Your Dream, The Reasons People Do Not Receive Their Financial Harvest and so forth.

Personally, I have a plan for every day of my life, every moment of my life.

When I am tired or need a change, I stop the plan and do something different for recreation for a couple of hours. But, I am very positive about what I want to do with my life.

But, I have friends who do not have any drive or passion to accomplish anything. Their goal is to pay their bills for the month. So, after they get paid, and they want to "have fun," they drop by my office. They want to talk. You see, they do not really respect the dreams of others. My goal is not vital to them. In fact, they will usually want to preach me a sermon on how I need to "relax." I am relaxed. I am happy. I do not need them in my life for relaxation. Sometimes these friends are a distraction. That is why you must pinpoint your own goals.

3. *Do Not Depend On Others To Inspire You Regarding Your Dreams.* Most will distract you. They do not value what you are pursuing. They do not celebrate what you are pursuing. You must name it for what it really is and move on with your life.

4. *You Must Determine What Your Goals Are Financially, Spiritually Or Physically.* Others cannot borrow your goals for themselves. You may have wonderful goals for those you love, but if they do not have the same dream for themselves, it is a waste of your time and energy.

Some years ago I purchased a special little

building for a physical fitness center for my staff. I was so excited. I hired a trainer to help each of my people develop their maximum level of health. It lasted less than a month. At the end of three weeks, only two people would show up at the special meeting with the trainer that was costing me $75 an hour. I was paying the trainer for them. But, they simply did not have any personal goals for themselves. The equipment was wasted. You simply cannot make others pursue worthwhile dreams for themselves.

5. *Avoid Intimate Relationships With People Who Disrespect Your Dreams.* You can minister to them. You can encourage them. You can speak words that strengthen and bless them. But, do not draw them close in or the burden will become too cumbersome and impossible for you to carry.

6. *Put Pictures Of Your Goals On Your Walls In Your Office, In Your Secret Place And On Your Refrigerator.* If you have a dream of losing weight, put pictures in front of you that inspire and excite you. Do you have a dream of owning your own home? Place a picture of it on the bulletin board at your home. What you keep looking at the most will influence your conversation and your faith.

7. *Write Out Your Dream On Paper.* "...Write the vision, and make it plain upon tables, that he may run that readeth it" (Hab. 2:2). A thought is not a plan. A wish is not a plan. A possibility is not a plan. True champions invest time and energy to develop a clear-cut written goal and dream. They plan for their life.

Always Pinpoint Your Goals.

It is one of the Golden Secrets of the Journey.

The Seed That Leaves
Your Hand Never Leaves
Your Life...But Enters Your
Future, Where It Multiplies.

-MIKE MURDOCK

≈ 3 ≈

NEVER SELL WHAT YOU ARE IN A POSITION TO SOW.

Your Decisions Multiply Or Subtract You.

Sometimes, you will have furniture, computers or clothes that you need to sell or get out of your house. You will be tempted to have a "garage sale" so that you can make a few hundred dollars extra. *Don't do it.*

Why spend 50 hours of your valuable time putting price tags on items, ads in the newspaper and two days of selling when you could sow? You see, I learned this the hard way.

Selling an item brings one price.

Sowing returns it 100 times (Mk. 10:28-30).

It happened to me a number of years ago. I had a wonderful computer. It served me well. But, as my ministry began to grow and mature, I needed something larger that could facilitate my letters to my partners. I had paid over $25,000 for the computer itself. However, when I asked the manufacturer what he would give me for the computer if I sold it back to him, he said, "$500."

I was very disappointed. Then, one of the staff members mentioned that a young preacher getting started could use it. He would be happy to pay me $500 or $1000 for the computer. Then, it dawned on me. *God was giving me an opportunity to plant a Seed.* Some might scoff and say that I was giving away used merchandise, that it was not my best. But, it was a great blessing to the young preacher that I sowed it into. He had nothing. Suddenly, he had the equipment he needed to birth his own next season.

Sowing opportunities occur often.

You have to *look* for them.

You may not have any extra cash today to plant. But, look around your closet. Rummage through your garage. You might have a refrigerator, an oven or some books that would bring great joy to a widow, a struggling young couple or a Bible school student.

You have *something* that can multiply.

But, no one can find it except you. It is your Harvest. It is *your* Seed. It is *your opportunity* to plant it instead of sell it.

When you solve a problem for someone, God solves a problem for you. Job discovered this. When he prayed for his friends, his own captivity was turned.

Here are some guidelines to help you find Seed to sow instead of something to sell:

1. *Anything you have not used during the last six months.* (Obviously, if you do not need something the first half of a year, you probably will not use it in the second half of the year. So, sow it! Somebody might be able to use it and desperately needs it even now.)

2. *Any item that doesn't bring you great joy.* Someone gave me a picture. I didn't enjoy it. Others

did. But, I did not want to place it on my walls of my home. A friend saw it in my garage and commented on it. I explained that I really did not have space, and it wasn't my kind of picture. My friend offered to purchase it from me. Instantly, I discerned the soil, *a place* I could sow a Seed. I refused to receive $50 or $60 for it. Instead, I sowed it as a Seed. (I probably don't have to really explain by now...other pictures have been sown into my life from other people since then over and *over again.*)

Business is a *trade-off.*

Sowing is a *trade-up.*

Business is exchanging something you own for something else you would prefer. Seed sowing is a different philosophy. Seed sowing is helping another person achieve their goal knowing that the Law of Multiplication will work for you when that person is not even present in your future.

Volunteers in ministries have learned this powerful secret. That explains their uncommon joy. As I have traveled for more than 35 years, I have noticed that volunteers are often much happier than employees.

Employees trade labor for a salary.

Volunteers sow their time for a future.

The difference in their joy, countenance and attitude is immediately noticeable. (Of course, there are exceptions to this rule, but this is something I notice everywhere.)

I never raise my prices on items when it is possible to lower them and still survive. I have been working on my next encyclopedia called, "The Uncommon Millionaire Encyclopedia." While studying the philosophy of Sam Walton, the multi-billionaire, I found some interesting things. Instead of trying to see how much money he could make customers pay, he worked with his manufacturers to see *how little he could possibly charge* and still survive. His success has not been equaled in America. He refused to raise a price if it was possible to survive by lowering it. His focus was the satisfaction and loyalty of customers. It has paid off remarkably.

It seems that I read a few days ago in a newspaper that Wal-Mart is the single largest employer in the United States today. "Bear ye one another's burdens...As we have therefore opportunity, let us do good unto all men, especially unto them who are of the household of faith" (Gal. 6:2,10).

Perhaps, this is the fascinating photograph in the mind of the Apostle Paul. He wrote, "...but, in lowliness of mind let each esteem other better than themselves. Look not every man on his own things, but every man also on the things of others" (Phil. 2:3,4).

Negotiation will take you far.

Sowing Seeds will take you further.

Never Sell What You Are In A Position To Sow.

It is one of the Secrets of the Journey.

≈ 4 ≈

ALWAYS SEE REJECTION AS A DOOR, NOT A WALL.

Rejection Is A Beginning, Not An End.
It is merely someone's opinion. Someone who is incapable of discerning your greatness.

Look at Walt Disney. Millions have enjoyed the incredible entertainment he has provided through Disney World. Who has been more creative on this earth than Walt Disney! But, there was a time in his life that his climate and situations did not inspire him. He was once fired by a newspaper because they felt he was "not creative enough." He knew rejection. They did not want him. He lost a job because of the opinions of others.

But, Disney saw rejection *as a door* to his next season. It was not a wall. It was not a conclusion. It was the entry into change.

Your loved ones may reject you. In his tremendous book, "The Salesman of the Century," Ron Popeil shares an encouraging note. His success is widely known. He has made millions in his presentations of inventions on television. Yet, he experienced feeling unloved. He writes, "Even though over the years I helped to make my father a richer man by selling his products on television, I still never got close to him. He never said he loved me...I never heard the word "love" from any of my relatives" (page 41). You see, he saw past their problem. He saw past their harshness. He *saw his future.*

Rejection cannot stop your future from emerging. Your unwillingness to persist can stop your future. So, make up your mind today to overcome every rejection you have experienced during your lifetime. Learn from it. Focus on something bigger than the opinions of others—your future success.

Your gifts and labors may be rejected. A number of years ago, Richard Bach wrote a ten thousand word story about a soaring seagull.

It was turned down by 18 publishers.

Finally, MacMillan published it in 1970. Within five years, by 1975, Jonathan Livingston Seagull had sold more than seven million copies in the United States alone.

Seven million copies after 18 rejections.

The opinions of others has nothing to do with your success. Their rejection can only affect your feelings, not your future.

What you discuss with others will become bigger. What you think about will multiply. Stop telling about your rejections. *Feed your dream until it becomes so big you cannot remember the rejection.*

Insist on overcoming rejection.

Always See Rejection As A Door, Not A Wall.

It is one of the Secrets of the Journey.

⬥ 5 ⬥

REMIND YOURSELF CONTINUOUSLY THAT OTHERS NEAR YOU ARE HURTING INSIDE.

Everyone Is Hiding Something.

It is not always because of deception. Neither are they trying to cover up something important.

Our wounds are simply private.

The things that make us cry often embarrass us. When a wife has received a harsh look from her husband, the pain goes too deep to discuss. When the husband hears the acid words from the love of his life, he comes apart *inside.* Yet, he cannot afford to show it. Neither can she. Nobody wants to look weak. So, every effort is made to shield ourselves, protect ourselves from the prying and often critical opinions of others.

So, nobody really sees how much *you hurt.*

I try to remind myself of this continuously. I fail a lot in it. Sometimes, if someone seems a little arrogant and aggressive, I will tend to confront them on that turf. I do not mind confrontation, since I think I am right most of the time! (Smile!) But, they are also thinking *they* are right!

Here is the problem.

You do not *really* know what is going on in another person's mind, therefore, it is important to continuously remind yourself that *others have painful experiences that they are not discussing with you or anyone else.*

Their decisions about everything are being made to *avoid the continuance* of that pain, thus repeating their failures. So, they will not make decisions totally based on what you are saying, your conversations. They are making decisions to move away from pain.

Every decision is to move away from perceived pain. Every decision is presumed to be an escape to pleasure, away from that pain.

When I remind myself of this, I am more gentle with people. More understanding. Less critical and harsh. Far more patient than I would normally be. You see, I want people to be patient with me too.

One of the secrets of the journey...is to continuously, *continuously* remind yourself that others are going *through trials you cannot see.*

They are crying tears you have never felt.

They are feeling isolated and rejected in ways you cannot imagine.

Don't become *another* burden to them.

Become *their Burden Bearer.*

When you telephone someone, ask yourself, "Am I calling to add to their burden *or to remove it?*"

When you write a letter, ask yourself, "Am I becoming *another* burden or their Burden Bearer?"

Maturity is the ability and willingness to bear the burdens of others.

Many years ago, I was in Fullerton, California.

The place was full of people. But, the service seemed very uptight and tense. Something was wrong. I almost became belligerent and told the people something every young evangelist normally tells the people.

"If you don't like what I'm preaching, stay home. The door swings both ways. I don't have to be here myself. I can leave town if I want to. I'm going to preach this gospel...no matter what you say. I'd rather preach under a tree by myself, than compromise this gospel." (Blah. Blah. Blah.)

But, Someone restrained me. (The Holy Spirit!)

After church, I discovered the reason for the terrible deathly atmosphere of the service. One of the main board members of the church had suddenly dropped dead that afternoon. Yet, his entire family had chosen to come sit in the service that night rather than go to the funeral home. They were so desperate for God to speak a word of comfort and strength to them, they came to the crusade.

Had I said what I felt—I would have doubled their pain and heartache. *Someone is always going through something you have not discerned.*

Listen to the Holy Spirit. Become intuitive. *Nothing Is Ever As It First Appears.*

Why did I remain composed and focused during the service, even though the church atmosphere was like death? I remembered *reading* a statement by a great preacher. He said every young preacher *"should always remember that on every pew sits at least one broken heart. Heal it."*

You will meet many people today. Many need kind words desperately.

Everyone hurts somewhere inside.

Most will not tell you about it. So, wrap your words with healing oil. You are their healer, sent by God.

You may be the only healer that crosses their path during their lifetime.

When you concentrate on the needs of others, God will focus on *your* needs. "Knowing that whatsoever good thing any man doeth, the same shall he receive of the Lord, whether he be bond or free" (Eph. 6:8).

Remind Yourself Continuously That Others Near You Are Hurting Inside.

That's one of the Secrets of the Journey.

≈ 6 ≈

ALWAYS STAY AWARE THAT THERE IS SOMETHING IN A SITUATION THAT YOU ARE NOT SEEING.

Your Struggles And Efforts Are Being Noted.
Someone is carefully evaluating your progress, pursuits and potential. You may not know the person. Perhaps you have not met him or her yet. It would astound you if you knew who is presently discussing your Assignment with great *favor* and appreciation.

This is very important. Your consistency is attracting attention. Your ability to stay *focused* is like a magnet. Somebody observing you now is considering entering your life with favor, influence and support. You will have access to their skills, Wisdom and circle of friendships, soon. "Seest thou a man diligent in his business? he shall stand before kings; he shall not stand before mean men" (Prov. 22:29).

People are *asking* about you. Your *endurance* is being admired. Your *integrity* is being mentioned in circles that would thrill and excite you. When these people enter your life, *you will achieve in a single day what would normally require a year for you to accomplish alone.*

Someone is carefully observing your productivity and attitude toward your present boss and superior.

It happened to Ruth. As you will recall, she was the Moabitess who gleaned in the fields of Boaz. She had followed her mother-in-law, Naomi, from Moab back to Bethlehem. Her father-in-law was dead. Her brother-in-law was dead. Her own husband was dead. She did not have any children. She was a lonely, focused and loyal peasant woman trying to find enough food to survive.

Someone noticed her. Boaz, the wealthy landowner, came to review the Harvest. He looked and saw Ruth. He said to his supervisor of reapers, "Whose damsel is this?" *The wealthy also study genealogies.* "...it is the Moabitish damsel that came back with Naomi out of the country of Moab: And she said, I pray you, let me glean and gather after the reapers among the sheaves: so she came, and hath continued even from the morning until now, that she tarried a little in the house" (Ruth 2:6,7).

Boaz approached Ruth. He explained that protection would be provided as long as she wanted to reap in his field. Her humility and sweet spirit had touched Boaz. Then Boaz explained that he knew who she was and who Naomi was. He confirmed that conversations had taken place concerning her life. "...It hath fully been showed me, all that thou hast done unto thy mother in law since the death of thine husband: and how thou hast left thy father and thy mother, and the land of thy nativity, and art come unto a people which thou knewest not heretofore" (Ruth 2:11).

Boldness is a quality every champion admires.

Oh, please listen to me today! You have no idea how many people are being stirred toward your life with great *favor.* Every good *Seed* that you have sown is going to grow and bear fruit. Every *hour* you have invested in restoring and healing others will produce an inevitable Harvest! *Your sacrifices are not in vain.* Your toils and struggles have been noted, *documented,* and observed by the Lord of the Harvest! "And let us not be weary in well doing: for in due season we shall reap, if we faint not" (Gal. 6:9).

The scenario then unfolds as Boaz invites Ruth to join his servants at meal time. She is permitted to sit beside the reaper. Boaz instructs his employees to leave extra barley for her. You see, the rich were instructed to leave the corners of their field for the poor and strangers to gather food for their own survival (see Lev. 19:9,10).

But here, Boaz has made a decision to leave plenty of barley accessible for Ruth. The Bible calls it, "handfuls of purpose," for her.

You see this kind of favor always occurs in the lives of those who are obsessed with their Assignment. *God goes before you.* He puts inside the hearts of others a desire to aid you, *assist you* and enable you to *complete your Assignment.* He is a just God. "The just Lord is in the midst thereof; He will not do iniquity: every morning doth He bring His judgment to light, He faileth not" (Zeph. 3:5).

Put excellence into your present. Do not wait for a glorious future to arrive. *Empty your best into your present.* Your present efforts are being multiplied, noticed and observed. Rewards are inevitable.

Picture this: you are running daily on the Track of Life. The grandstand of spectators is observing you—*far more than you could possibly know.* "Wherefore seeing we also are compassed about with so great a cloud of witnesses, let us lay aside every weight, and the sin which doth so easily beset us, and let us run with patience the race that is set before us" (Heb. 12:1).

Run today with excellence.

Someone is watching who may be the Golden Bridge to your next season.

Always Stay Aware That There Is Someone In A Situation That You Are Not Seeing.

It is one of the Secrets of the Journey.

⚕ 7 ⚕

SOW PROPORTIONATE TO THE HARVEST YOU DESIRE.

━━━━►❋◄━━━━

The Size Of Your Seed Determines The Size Of Your Harvest.

The Apostle Paul made this clear, "...he which soweth sparingly shall reap also sparingly; and he which soweth bountifully shall reap also bountifully" (2 Cor. 9:6).

I will never forget an experience in the Northeast. A large lady moved toward me after service.

"I'm believing God to make me a millionaire. And, I believe it will happen within 12 months. Here's my Seed to make it happen." She thrust something into my hand. I looked at her and said, "I am believing God with you."

After she walked away, I opened my hand. It was a crumpled dollar bill. *A dollar bill.*

Now there is nothing wrong with sowing a small Seed. Everything must have a *beginning* point. Jesus commended the woman who gave a small offering—*because it was all she had.* He said that she gave more than anyone else present that day.

But, Jesus did not say that her small offering

was necessarily going to make her a millionaire. You see, your Seed must be comparable to the Harvest you are sowing toward.

You cannot plant a Chevrolet Seed and produce a Rolls Royce Harvest. This was what Paul was teaching. If you sow small, you will still reap. But, it will not be a large Harvest.

Millions have not grasped this. They continue to roll up dollar bills, drop them in the offering plate, and hope no one watches. Yet, they are writing their prayer requests as if they are expecting Cadillacs, yachts and million dollar homes.

You can *begin* with a small Seed. When God begins to bless that small Seed, you must increase the size of the Seed if you want the Harvest to increase.

You must learn to move from glory to glory.

I told about an incredible miracle in my life one night. I was sitting in a beautiful Mustang convertible—teal bottom and white top. Gorgeous. It had "fun" written all over the car!

"I just bought this car this week," my friend explained. "However, I decided that I want a jeep instead. Do you think you might want to buy this car from me?"

"I think I may!" was my reply.

The next day, we pulled up at a service station. After he filled the tank, he went inside to pay the bill. I began to pray "in the Spirit." Suddenly, I began to feel a faith rise up in me for him to sow the car as a Seed into my life! Now, that sounds a little crazy. But, I began to pray intensely. When he got back in the car, he looked at me. He cocked his head sideways and said, "You really like this car?"

"I *love* this car," I gushed.

"Your ministry has so affected and blessed me, I have been wondering what I could do to bless you." He handed me the keys with a smile. The car was mine. Free. An incredible gift that will stay in my heart forever.

When I was in a crusade later, I shared this story. I told everyone that I was going to pray that the mantle of favor would come upon their life. *One Day Of Favor Is Worth A Thousand Days Of Labor.* When God wants to bless you, He puts somebody close to you who cares about your life and needs.

A young man approached me after church a little disgruntled. Agitated. Frustrated.

"I did that already and it did not work," he explained. "I planted a Seed several months ago and I have never had a car given to me. I need transportation. Why didn't it work for me?"

"Have you ever planted a car in the life of someone else?" I asked.

"No, I have not," was his hesitant and reluctant reply.

"I have. That's why my faith worked for me. I had already *planted* a car and I had every right and ability to *expect* one to be given back to me," I explained.

You cannot "faith" *into* your life what you have not "faithed" *away* from your life.

You will only have the faith to call in toward your life something that you have sowed out.

Your faith works the most, the strongest when you have planted a Seed comparable to the Harvest you desire.

When you are willing to work with the different levels of your faith and sow Seed proportionately, you will be amazed at the changes that will happen in your financial prosperity.

Sow Proportionate To The Harvest You Desire. *It is one of the Secrets of the Journey.*

DECISION

Will You Accept Jesus As Your Personal Savior Today?

The Bible says, "That if thou shalt confess with thy mouth the Lord Jesus, and shalt believe in thine heart that God hath raised Him from the dead, thou shalt be saved" (Rom. 10:9).

Pray this prayer from your heart today!

"Dear Jesus, I believe that You died for me and rose again on the third day. I confess I am a sinner...I need Your love and forgiveness... Come into my heart. Forgive my sins. I receive your eternal life. Confirm Your love by giving me peace, joy and supernatural love for others. Amen."

DR. MIKE MURDOCK

is in tremendous demand as one of the most dynamic speakers in America today.

More than 14,000 audiences in 38 countries have attended his meetings and seminars. Hundreds of invitations come to him from churches, colleges and business corporations. He is a noted author of over 130 books, including the best sellers, *"The Leadership Secrets of Jesus"* and *"Secrets of the Richest Man Who Ever Lived."* Thousands view his weekly television program, *"Wisdom Keys with Mike Murdock."* Many attend his Saturday School of Wisdom Breakfasts that he hosts in major cities of America.

☐ Yes, Mike! I made a decision to accept Christ as my personal Savior today. Please send me my free gift of your book, *"31 Keys to a New Beginning"* to help me with my new life in Christ. *(B-48)*

NAME   BIRTHDAY

ADDRESS

CITY   STATE   ZIP

PHONE   E-MAIL   *B-103*

Mail form to:
The Wisdom Center • P. O. Box 99 • Denton, TX 76202
Phone: 1-888-WISDOM-1 (1-888-947-3661)
*Website: **www.thewisdomcenter.cc***

Will You Become A Wisdom Key Partner?

The Assignment Of This Ministry Is To Pursue, Proclaim And Publish The Wisdom Of God.

1. **Television & Radio** - *"Wisdom Keys With Mike Murdock,"* a nationally-syndicated weekly television program features Mike Murdock's teaching and music.

2. **The Wisdom Center** - The Ministry offices where Dr. Murdock holds an annual School of Wisdom for those desiring The Uncommon Life.

3. **Missionary Ministry** - Dr. Murdock's overseas outreaches to 38 countries have included crusades in East and West Africa, South America and Europe.

4. **Music Ministry** - Millions of people have been blessed by the anointed songwriting and singing of Mike Murdock, who has made over 15 music albums and CDs available.

5. **Wisdom Books & Literature** - Over 120 best-selling Wisdom Books and 70 Teaching Tape Series.

6. **Church Crusades** - Multitudes are ministered to in crusades and seminars throughout America in "The Mike Murdock School Of Wisdom." Known as a man who loves pastors has focused on church crusades for 36 years.

7. **Schools of Wisdom** - In 24 major cities Mike Murdock hosts Saturday Schools of Wisdom for those who want personalized and advanced training for achieving "The Uncommon Life."

8. **Schools of the Holy Spirit** - Mike Murdock hosts Schools of the Holy Spirit in many churches to mentor believers on the Person and companionship of the Holy Spirit.

I want to personally invite you to be a part of this ministry!

WISDOM KEY PARTNERSHIP PLAN

Dear Partner,

God has connected us.

Will you become a Wisdom Key Faith Partner with my ministry? Your monthly Seeds are so powerful in helping heal broken lives. When you sow into the work of God, four Miracle Harvests are guaranteed in Scripture:

▶ Uncommon Protection (Mal. 3:10,11)

▶ Uncommon Favor (Lk. 6:38)

▶ Uncommon Health (Isa. 58:8)

▶ Uncommon Financial Ideas and Wisdom (Deut. 8:18)

Your Faith Partner,

Mike Murdock

Clip and Mail

❑ Yes, Mike, I want to be a Wisdom Key Partner with you. Please rush The Wisdom Key Partnership Pak to me today!

❑ **Y**es, Mike, I want to be a Wisdom Key Monthly Partner. Enclosed is my first monthly Seed-Faith Promise of $_____.   Total Enclosed $ _____

Name _____ Birthdate ___/___

Address _____

City _____ State _____ Zip _____

Phone (____)_____ E-Mail _____

B-103

Mail To:

The Wisdom Center · P.O. Box 99 · Denton, TX 76202

1-888-WISDOM-1 (1-888-947-3661)

Website: **www.thewisdomcenter.cc**

WISDOM KEY BOOKS

Cat. #	No. Ea.	Wisdom Key Books $3.00 each book	Total Price
B02		Five Steps Out Of Depression	
B03		The Sex Trap	
B04		Ten Lies Many People Believe About Money	
B05		Finding Your Purpose In Life	
B06		Creating Tomorrow Through Seed-Faith	
B07		Battle Techniques For War Weary Saints	
B08		Enjoying the Winning Life	
B09		Four Forces That Guarantee Career Success	
B10		The Bridge Called Divorce	
B55		20 Keys To A Happier Marriage	
B56		How To Turn Mistakes Into Miracles	
B64		Seven Obstacles To Abundant Success	
B65		Born To Taste The Grapes	
B66		Greed, Gold and Giving	
B69		Wisdom Keys For A Powerful Prayer Life	
B80		The Greatest Success Habit On Earth	
		Total Items Ordered Sub Total	
		Add 10% Shipping	
		Total Enclosed	

Name _____

Address _____

City _____ State _____ Zip _____

☐ Visa   ☐ AMEX   ☐ MC   Expiration Date _____

☐ Discover   ☐ Money Order   ☐ Cash   ☐ Check

Card # _____

Authorized Signature _____

Mail To:
The Wisdom Center *· P.O. Box 99 · Denton, TX 76202*
1-888-WISDOM-1 (1-888-947-3661)
Website: ***www.thewisdomcenter.cc***

Clip and Mail

WISDOM 12 PAK

THE MASTER SECRET OF LIFE IS WISDOM
Ignorance Is The Only True Enemy Capable Of Destroying You (Hosea 4:6, Proverbs 11:14)

▸ 1.	MY PERSONAL DREAM BOOK	B143	$5.00
▸ 2.	THE COVENANT OF FIFTY-EIGHT BLESSINGS	B47	$8.00
▸ 3.	WISDOM, GOD'S GOLDEN KEY TO SUCCESS	B71	$7.00
▸ 4.	SEEDS OF WISDOM ON THE HOLY SPIRIT	B116	$5.00
▸ 5.	SEEDS OF WISDOM ON THE SECRET PLACE	B115	$5.00
▸ 6.	SEEDS OF WISDOM ON THE WORD OF GOD	B117	$5.00
▸ 7.	SEEDS OF WISDOM ON YOUR ASSIGNMENT	B122	$5.00
▸ 8.	SEEDS OF WISDOM ON PROBLEM SOLVING	B118	$5.00
▸ 9.	101 WISDOM KEYS	B45	$7.00
▸ 10.	31 KEYS TO A NEW BEGINNING	B48	$7.00
▸ 11.	THE PROVERBS 31 WOMAN	B49	$7.00
▸ 12.	31 FACTS ABOUT WISDOM	B46	$7.00

Wisdom Is The Principal Thing

Book Pak
WBL-12 **/$30**
(A $73 Value!)

The Wisdom Center

ORDER TODAY!
www.thewisdomcenter.cc

1-888-WISDOM-1
(1-888-947-3661)

THE WISDOM CENTER • P.O. Box 99 • Denton, Texas 76202

33

Money Matters.

This Powerful Video will unleash the Financial Harvest of your lifetime!

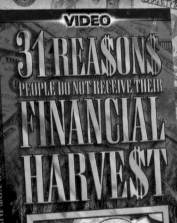

VIDEO

31 REAON
PEOPLE DO NOT RECEIVE THEIR
FINANCIAL HARVE$T

MIKE MURDOCK

▶ 8 Scriptural Reasons You Should Pursue Financial Prosperity

▶ The Secret Prayer Key You Need When Making A Financial Request To God

▶ The Weapon Of Expectation And The 5 Miracles It Unlocks

▶ How To Discern Those Who Qualify To Receive Your Financial Assistance

▶ How To Predict The Miracle Moment God Will Schedule Your Financial Breakthrough

Wisdom Is The Principal Thing

Video VI-17 / **$30**

Six Audio Tapes / **$30** TS-71

Book / **$12** B-82

The Wisdom Center

ORDER TODAY!
www.thewisdomcenter.cc

1-888-WISDOM-1
(1-888-947-3661)

THE WISDOM CENTER • P.O. Box 99 • Denton, Texas 76202

34

The Secret To 1000 Times More.

In this Dynamic Video you will find answers to unleash Financial Flow into your life!

VIDEO

7 KEYS to 1000 TIMES MORE

7 KEYS to 1000 TIMES MORE

The Lord God Of Your Fathers Make You A Thousand Times So Many More As You Are, And Bless You, As He Hath Promised You!
Deuteronomy 1:11

MIKE MURDOCK

▶ **Habits Of Uncommon Achievers**

▶ **The Greatest Success Law I Ever Discovered**

▶ **How To Discern Your Place Of Assignment, The Only Place Financial Provision Is Guaranteed**

▶ **3 Secret Keys In Solving Problems For Others**

▶ **How To Become The Next Person To Receive A Raise On Your Job**

Wisdom Is The Principal Thing
Video VI-16 / **$30**
Six Audio Tapes / **$30** TS-104
Book / **$10** B-104
The Wisdom Center

ORDER TODAY! 1-888-WISDOM-1
www.thewisdomcenter.cc (1-888-947-3661)

THE WISDOM CENTER • P.O. Box 99 • Denton, Texas 76202

35

Somebody's Future
Will Not Begin Until You Enter.

THIS COLLECTION INCLUDES 4 DIFFERENT BOOKS CONTAINING
UNCOMMON WISDOM FOR DISCOVERING YOUR LIFE ASSIGNMENT

▶ How To Achieve A God-Given Dream And Goal

▶ How To Know Who Is Assigned To You

▶ The Purpose And Rewards Of An Enemy

Wisdom Is The Principal Thing
Book Pak
WBL-14 /$30
Buy 3-Get 1 Free
($10 Each/$40 Value!)
The Wisdom Center

36

The Secret Place

Library Pak

Songs From The Secret Place

Over 40 Great Songs On 6 Music Tapes
Including "I'm In Love" / Love Songs From The Holy Spirit
Birthed In The Secret Place / <u>Side A</u> Is Dr. Mike Murdock
Singing / <u>Side B</u> Is Music Only For Your Personal Prayer Time

Seeds Of Wisdom On The Secret Place

4 Secrets The Holy Spirit Reveals In The Secret Place /
The Necessary Ingredients In Creating Your Secret Place /
10 Miracles That Will Happen In The Secret Place

Seeds Of Wisdom On The Holy Spirit

The Protocol For Entering The Presence Of The Holy Spirit /
The Greatest Day Of My Life And What Made It So /
Power Keys For Developing Your Personal Relationship With The Holy Spirit

Wisdom Is The Principal Thing
Book/Tape Pak
SP PAK-001 /$30
Six Audio Tapes & Two Books
(A $40 Value!)
The Wisdom Center

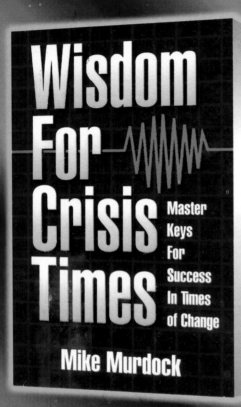

The SCHOOL of WISDOM

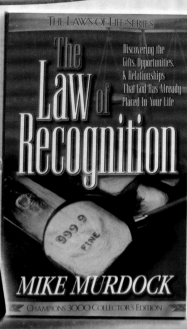

▶ 47 Keys In Recognizing The Mate God Has Approved For You

▶ 14 Facts You Should Know About Your Gifts and Talents

▶ 17 Important Facts You Should Remember About Your Weakness

▶ And Much, Much More...

▶ What Attracts Others Toward You

▶ The Secret Of Multiplying Your Financial Blessings

▶ What Stops The Flow Of Your Faith

▶ Why Some Fail And Others Succeed

▶ How To Discern Your Life Assignment

▶ How To Create Currents Of Favor With Others

▶ How To Defeat Loneliness

Wisdom Is The Principal Thing

Book/Tape Pak
PAK-002 / $30
Six Audio Tapes & Book
(A $40 Value!)
The Wisdom Center

Learn From The Greatest.

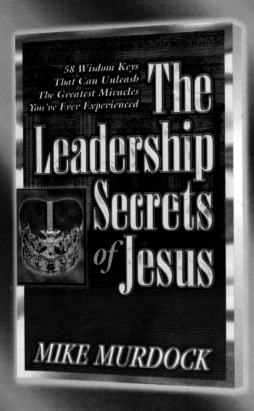

- ▶ The Secret Of Handling Rejection
- ▶ How To Deal With The Mistakes Of Others
- ▶ 5 Power Keys For Effective Delegation To Others
- ▶ The Key To Developing Great Faith
- ▶ The Greatest Qualities Of Champions
- ▶ The Secret Of The Wealthy
- ▶ 4 Goal-Setting Techniques
- ▶ 10 Facts Jesus Taught About Money

In this dynamic and practical guidebook Mike Murdock points you directly to Jesus, the Ultimate Mentor. You'll take just a moment every day to reflect on His life and actions. And when you do, you'll discover all the key skills and traits that Jesus used... the powerful "leadership secrets" that build true, lasting achievement. Explore them. Study them. Put them to work in your own life and your success will be assured!

Wisdom Is The Principal Thing

Book B-91 / **$10**

The Wisdom Center

Your Rewards In Life Are Determined By The Problems You Solve.

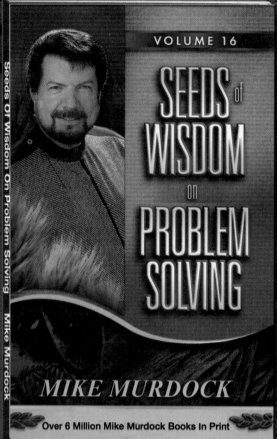

- ▶ 3 Simple Ways To Increase Your Income In 90 Days

- ▶ 4 Keys To Recognizing The Problems You Were Created To Solve

- ▶ 12 Rewards Received When You Solve Problems For Others

- ▶ 5 Important Keys To Remember When You Face A Problem

- ▶ 2 Ways You Will Be Remembered

- ▶ 12 Keys to Becoming An Uncommon Problem Solver

- ▶ 6 Keys To Establishing Your Legacy

Wisdom Is The Principal Thing

Book B-118 / $5

The Wisdom Center

You Can Have It.

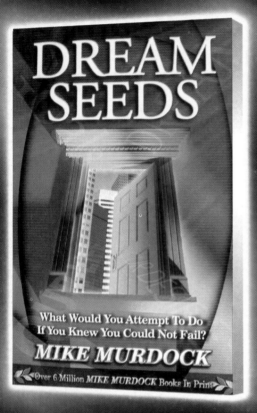

DREAM SEEDS

What Would You Attempt To Do If You Knew You Could Not Fail?

MIKE MURDOCK

Over 6 Million *MIKE MURDOCK* Books In Print

- ▸ Why Sickness Is Not The Will Of God
- ▸ How To Release The Powerful Forces That Guarantee Blessing
- ▸ The Incredible Role Of Your Memory And The Imagination
- ▸ The Hidden Power Of Imagination And How To Use It Properly
- ▸ The Difference Between The Love Of God And His Blessings
- ▸ 3 Steps In Increasing Your Faith
- ▸ 2 Rewards That Come When You Use Your Faith In God
- ▸ 7 Powerful Keys Concerning Your Faith

Dreams and desires begin as photographs within our hearts and minds – things that we want to happen in our future. God plants these pictures as invisible Seeds within us. God begins every miracle in your life with a Seed-picture... the invisible idea that gives birth to a visible blessing. In this teaching, you will discover your desires and how to concentrate on watering and nurturing the growth of your Dream-Seeds until you attain your God-given goals.

Wisdom Is The Principal Thing

Book B-11 / **$9**

Six Audio Tapes TS-2 / **$30**

The Wisdom Center

Where You Are Determines What Grows In You.

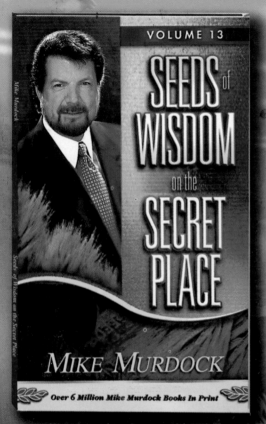

- ▸ 4 Secrets The Holy Spirit Reveals In The Secret Place

- ▸ Master Keys In Cultivating An Effective Prayer Life

- ▸ The Necessary Ingredients In Creating Your Secret Place

- ▸ 10 Miracles That Will Happen In The Secret Place

Wisdom Is The Principal Thing

Book B-115 / $5

The Wisdom Center

Run To Win.

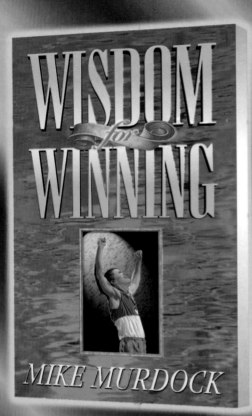

MIKE MURDOCK

▶ 10 Ingredients For Success

▶ 10 Lies Many People Believe About Money

▶ 20 Keys For Winning At Work

▶ 20 Keys To A Better Marriage

▶ 3 Facts Every Parent Should Remember

▶ 5 Steps Out Of Depression

▶ The Greatest Wisdom Principle I Ever Learned

▶ 7 Keys To Answered Prayer

▶ God's Master Golden Key To Total Success

▶ The Key To Understanding Life

Everyone needs to feel they have achieved something with their life. When we stop producing, loneliness and laziness will choke all enthusiasm from our living. What would you like to be doing? What are you doing about it? Get started on a project in your life. Start building on your dreams. Resist those who would control and change your personal goals. Get going with this powerful teaching and reach your life goals!

Wisdom Is The Principal Thing

Book B-01 / $10

Six Audio Tapes TS-01 / $30

The Wisdom Center

THE SECRET.

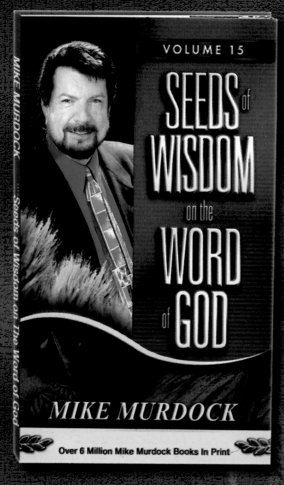

VOLUME 15

SEEDS of **WISDOM** on the **WORD** of **GOD**

MIKE MURDOCK

Over 6 Million Mike Murdock Books In Print

- ▸ 11 Reasons Why The Bible Is The Most Important Book On Earth

- ▸ 12 Problems The Word Of God Can Solve In Your Life

- ▸ 4 Of My Personal Bible Reading Secrets

- ▸ 4 Steps To Building A Spiritual Home

- ▸ 9 Wisdom Keys To Being Successful In Developing The Habit Of Reading The Word Of God

Wisdom Is The Principal Thing

Book B-117 / $5

The Wisdom Center

WISDOM COLLECTION

8

SECRETS OF THE UNCOMMON MILLIONAIRE

1. The Uncommon Millionaire Conference Vol. 1 (Six Cassettes)
2. The Uncommon Millionaire Conference Vol. 2 (Six Cassettes)
3. The Uncommon Millionaire Conference Vol. 3 (Six Cassettes)
4. The Uncommon Millionaire Conference Vol. 4 (Six Cassettes)
5. 31 Reasons People Do Not Receive Their Financial Harvest (256 Page Book)
6. Secrets of the Richest Man Who Ever Lived (178 Page Book)
7. 12 Seeds Of Wisdom Books On 12 Topics
8. The Gift Of Wisdom For Leaders Desk Calendar
9. 101 Wisdom Keys On Tape (Audio Tape)
10. In Honor Of The Holy Spirit (Music Cassette)
11. 365 Memorization Scriptures On The Word Of God (Audio Cassette)

Wisdom Is The Principal Thing

THE WISDOM COLLECTION 8
SECRETS OF THE UNCOMMON MILLIONAIRE

WC-08 / **$195**

The Wisdom Center

The Wisdom Center

ORDER TODAY!
www.thewisdomcenter.cc

1-888-WISDOM-1
(1-888-947-3661)

THE WISDOM CENTER • P.O. Box 99 • Denton, Texas 76202

47

The Secrets For Surviving.